D1489574

Baby animals in water habitats

Bobbie
Kalman

🌳 Crabtree Publishing Company
www.crabtreebooks.com

Created by Bobbie Kalman

For Grace Filomena
with love from your Auntie Bobbie
Do you like the baby animals in this book?

Author and Editor-in-Chief
Bobbie Kalman

Editors
Kathy Middleton
Crystal Sikkens

Design
Bobbie Kalman
Katherine Berti
Samantha Crabtree
(cover)

Photo research
Bobbie Kalman

Print and production coordinator
Katherine Berti

Prepress technician
Katherine Berti

Illustrations
Bonna Rouse: page 8

Photographs
Adobe Image Library: page 7 (top right)
Creatas: page 21 (top)
Digital Vision: page 15 (bottom right)
Photodisc: page 5 (raccoons)
Photos.com: pages 18, 24 (middle right)
Shutterstock: front and back covers and
 all other photographs
Wikipedia: Mike Baird: pages 12 (sea otters),
 24 (top right)

Library and Archives Canada Cataloguing in Publication

Kalman, Bobbie, 1947-
    Baby animals in water habitats / Bobbie Kalman.

(The habitats of baby animals)
Includes index.
Issued also in electronic format.
ISBN 978-0-7787-7734-2 (bound).--ISBN 978-0-7787-7747-2 (pbk.)

    1. Aquatic animals--Infancy--Juvenile literature. 2. Aquatic
ecology--Juvenile literature. I. Title. II. Series: Kalman, Bobbie, 1947- .
Habitats of baby animals.

QL120.K34 2011   j591.3'909169   C2011-902559-0

Library of Congress Cataloging-in-Publication Data

Kalman, Bobbie.
  Baby animals in water habitats / Bobbie Kalman.
    p. cm. -- (The habitats of baby animals)
  Includes index.
  ISBN 978-0-7787-7734-2 (reinforced library binding : alk. paper) --
ISBN 978-0-7787-7747-2 (pbk. : alk. paper) -- ISBN 978-1-4271-9718-4
(electronic pdf)
  1. Aquatic animals--Infancy--Juvenile literature. 2. Aquatic animals--
Ecology--Juvenile literature. I. Title.
  QL120.K35 2012
  591.76--dc22
                                                    2011013875

Crabtree Publishing Company

www.crabtreebooks.com   1-800-387-7650

Printed in China/082011/TM20110511

Published in Canada
Crabtree Publishing
616 Welland Ave.
St. Catharines, Ontario
L2M 5V6

Published in the United States
Crabtree Publishing
PMB 59051
350 Fifth Avenue, 59th Floor
New York, New York 10118

Published in the United Kingdom
Crabtree Publishing
Maritime House
Basin Road North, Hove
BN41 1WR

Published in Australia
Crabtree Publishing
386 Mt. Alexander Rd.
Ascot Vale (Melbourne)
VIC 3032

What is in this book?

Water on Earth

A **habitat** is a place in nature. Plants and animals live in habitats. There are habitats on land and in water. Water covers about three-quarters of Earth. **Oceans** are huge areas of water. The water in oceans is **salt water**. Salt water contains a lot of salt.

There are five oceans on Earth. From largest to smallest, they are the Pacific Ocean, Atlantic Ocean, Indian Ocean, Southern Ocean, and Arctic Ocean.

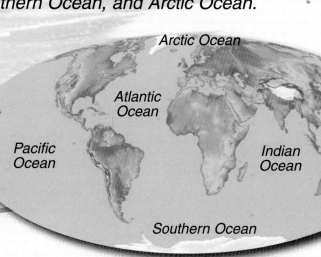

Arctic Ocean

Atlantic Ocean

Pacific Ocean

Pacific Ocean

Indian Ocean

Southern Ocean

This raccoon mother and her baby are getting a drink and looking for food in water.

Fresh water

Some water habitats contain **fresh water**. Fresh water does not have very much salt. In the picture above, the raccoon mother and her **kit**, or baby, are in a **pond**. A pond is a small **lake**. A lake is a body of water with land all around it. It is a freshwater habitat.

Water for life

Plants, animals, and people are **living things**. Living things grow, change, and make new living things. Water is a **non-living** thing. All living things need water to grow and stay healthy. Plants cannot grow without water. Animals and people cannot live without water. Water is everywhere! It is in oceans, lakes, ponds, **rivers**, and **wetlands**. It is under the ground. It is in the air. It is in clouds.

These plants are growing in water.
This baby alligator lives in water.

Animals need to drink water. These hyena pups have found water to drink.

Animals find food in water. These bear cubs are learning to catch fish in a river.

Animals take baths in water. They also use water to keep cool in the hot sun. This elephant mother is giving her **calf**, or baby, a cold shower.

Food in water

Animals need **energy**, or power, to breathe, move, grow, and stay alive. They get their energy from eating other living things. Plants make their own food from air, water, and sunlight. The leaves of water plants grow above water to catch the sunlight they need to make food. Making food from sunlight is called **photosynthesis**.

The leaves of plants take in air and sunlight. Food is made in the leaves.

The roots of plants take in water. Roots grow in soil under water.

A food chain

Animals that live in water habitats find plenty of food to eat. Some animals eat mainly plants. Plant-eaters are called **herbivores**. Animals that eat other animals are called **carnivores**. **Omnivores** eat both plants and other animals. When an animal eats another animal that has eaten a plant, there is a **food chain**. This freshwater food chain is made up of a flower, a butterfly, and a frog.

1. Plants make their own food. They contain the sun's energy.

*2. A butterfly drinks **nectar**. Nectar is a sweet liquid found in the flowers of some plants. When the butterfly drinks the nectar, some of the sun's energy is passed along to the butterfly.*

3. When the frog eats the butterfly, some of the sun's energy is passed from the plant to the butterfly and then to the frog.

sun

①

②

③

9

Water babies

raccoon kit

Many animals live in more than one kind of water habitat. Some spend all their time in water. Others spend time both in water and on land. Some of the baby animals that live in or beside water habitats are shown on these pages. One of these can live only in water. Which one is it? (See page 15 if you do not know.)

duckling

gosling (baby goose)

alligator hatchling

baby nutria

froglet

cygnet
(baby swan)

otter pup

dolphin mother

dolphin calf

tiger cub

fawn
(baby deer)

hippo calves

11

Animal mothers

Many kinds of animals live in water habitats. Some are **mammals**. Mammals are animals with hair or fur. They are born live. Most mammal mothers take care of their babies for a long time. After their babies are born, they feed them milk from their bodies. Drinking mother's milk is called **nursing**.

*Sea otters live on some **coasts** of the Pacific Ocean. Coasts are land areas at the edges of oceans. Other otters live in rivers. Otters are mammals. They have fur on their bodies, and the mothers feed their babies milk. This sea otter pup is nursing.*

Bird parents

Bird mothers also take care of their babies. Mother birds lay eggs, from which baby birds **hatch**, or come out. Many bird fathers help build nests and feed the babies.

These birds are great blue herons. They live in wetlands (see pages 22–23).

13

Baby ocean animals

Some of the baby animals that live in oceans are sea turtles, dolphins, whales, penguins, seals, and many kinds of fish. Fish, whales, and dolphins spend all their time in the water. Sea turtles, seals, and penguins spend some time on land.

sponge

sponge

This baby hawksbill sea turtle started its life on land. It lives in an ocean and eats sponges. A sponge is a simple animal that is attached to a location in the water and cannot move.

This baby dolphin holds its head above the water to breathe, but it cannot live out of water.

Baby penguins hatch from eggs on land. They find food in water.

This baby tiger shark is swimming at the edge of the ocean, but it cannot come onto land.

Babies in lakes

Lakes are large bodies of fresh water with land around them. The water in many lakes is **still** and deep. Still water does not move very much. Many animals live in lakes and raise their babies there because they can find both food and water. Lakes are full of plants, fish, and other animals.

This baby hippo lives in a lake. It stays in water all day to keep its skin from burning in the sun. At night, it leaves the water with its mother and eats grasses on land.

Baby birds

Many birds that live in places with cold winters **migrate**, or travel, to warmer places in autumn. They return in the spring to lay eggs and raise their babies. They live beside lakes and raise their babies both in water and on land. They eat plants that grow in water and grasses that grow on land. Some eat fish, insects, and other animals.

This Canada goose is swimming on a lake with her goslings.

These goslings are eating some grasses on land.

Cygnets sometimes ride on their mother's back to feel safe. Riding on their mother's back also keeps them warm.

Babies in ponds

Ponds are small lakes with shallow, still water. Plants grow in ponds and around their edges. Some animals eat parts of the plants, and some birds use them to make nests. Dragonflies lay their eggs on the leaves. Frogs grow in pond water and sit on pond plants to warm themselves in the sun. Ponds are busy places!

This mother grebe has built a nest for her chicks on a pond.

3. froglet

2. tadpole

1. frog eggs

4. adult frog

Frogs lay their eggs in ponds. A tadpole hatches from each egg. A tadpole grows legs and becomes a froglet. When the froglet loses its tail, it is an adult frog.

eggs

Dragonflies lay their eggs on pond plants.

River babies

A river is a body of water that flows from higher to lower places. As rivers flow, they carry fresh water to plants, animals, and people. Many animals live in river habitats. Frogs, turtles, and ducks live on rivers and along the **banks** of rivers. A bank is land at the edge of a river. Other animals visit rivers to cool their bodies, to find food to eat, and to drink fresh water.

This mother river otter has caught a fish. She will share some of the fish with her pup.

Tigers are powerful swimmers and spend a lot of time in rivers. This mother tiger is showing her cub how to find fish and turtles to eat.

Nutrias are **rodents**. Rodents have four front teeth that never stop growing. Nutrias often build their homes into the soft mud of riverbanks. Their homes can have entrances in the ground or in the water.

Babies in wetlands

A wetland is land that is covered with water for all or part of the year. Wetlands are very important habitats. They provide animals with places to live and raise their young. They are also important places for migrating birds to stop for a drink of water and to find food. There are two main kinds of wetlands. They are **swamps** and **marshes**.

Swamps are wetlands with trees. They are covered with water for part of the year. Swamps that are close to oceans contain salt water. Swamps that are far from oceans contain fresh water. Crocodiles, alligators, turtles, snakes, and many kinds of birds live among the trees that grow in swamps. This alligator lives in a swamp.

What are marshes?

Marshes are shallow, grassy wetlands without trees. They are covered with water all year. Marshes are found along the edges of lakes, rivers, and ponds. Raccoons, otters, frogs, and deer are just a few of the animals that live in marshes. Many birds also make nests in marshes.

This marsh warbler father is feeding his chicks in the nest.

This white-tailed deer mother and her fawn are having a drink of water. There is plenty of water to drink and plants to eat in this marsh.

Words to know and Index

nursing

food
pages 5, 7, 8,
9, 12, 15, 16,
17, 20, 22, 23

food chain
page 9

lake
pages 5, 6,
16–17, 18, 23

mothers
pages 5, 7, 11, 12–13,
16, 17, 18, 20, 21, 23

oceans
pages 4, 6, 12,
14–15, 22

pond
pages 5, 6, 18–19, 23

Other index words
babies pages 5, 6, 7,
10–11, 12, 13, 14, 15,
16, 17, 18, 20, 21, 22, 23
carnivores page 9
fresh water pages 5, 9,
16, 20, 22
habitats pages 4, 5, 9,
10, 12, 20, 22
herbivores page 9
living things pages 6, 8
non-living things page 6
omnivores page 9
photosynthesis page 8
plants pages 4, 6, 8, 9,
16, 17, 18, 19, 20, 23
salt water pages 4, 22

rivers
pages 6, 7, 12,
20–21, 23

wetlands
pages 6, 13, 22–23